It's fun to draw
Farm Animals

Mark Bergin

SKY PONY PRESS
NEW YORK

Mark Bergin was born in Hastings, England. He has illustrated an award-winning series and written over twenty books. He has done many book designs, layouts, and storyboards in many styles including cartoon for numerous books, posters, and advertisements. He lives in Bexhill-on-sea with his wife and three children.

HOW TO USE THIS BOOK:

Start by following the numbered splats on the left-hand page. These steps will ask you to add some lines to your drawing. The new lines are always drawn in red so you can see how the drawing builds from step to step. Read the "You can do it!" splats to learn about drawing and coloring techniques you can use.

Sky Pony Press books may be purchased in bulk at special discounts for sales promotion, corporate gifts, fund-raising, or educational purposes. Special editions can also be created to specifications. For details, contact the Special Sales Department, Sky Pony Press, 307 West 36th Street, 11th Floor, New York, NY 10018 or info@skyhorsepublishing.com.

Sky Pony® is a registered trademark of Skyhorse Publishing, Inc.®, a Delaware corporation.

Visit our website at www.skyponypress.com.

10 9 8 7 6 5 4 3 2 1

Manufactured in China, March 2012
This product conforms to CPSIA 2008

Library of Congress Cataloging-in-Publication Data

Bergin, Mark, 1961-
  It's fun to draw farm animals / Mark Bergin.
    pages cm
  Includes index.
  ISBN 978-1-61608-669-5 (pbk. : alk. paper)
  1. Domestic animals in art--Juvenile literature. 2. Livestock in art--Juvenile literature. 3. Drawing--Technique--Juvenile literature. I. Title.
  NC783.8.D65B473 2012
                    2012012966

ISBN: 978-1-61608-669-5

Contents

Chicken

1 Start with the head. Add a dot for the eye.

2 Add the beak and head details.

3 Add the body.

4 Draw in a wing and tail feathers.

you can do it!

Use oil pastels and smudge them with your finger. Use a felt-tip marker for the lines.

splat-a-fact

Male chickens are larger and more brightly colored than females.

5 Draw in two legs and feet.

4

Cow

1 start with the head and add two rounded shapes.

2 Add the eyes, nostrils, ears, and horns.

3 Draw in the body.

4 Add four legs and hooves.

5 Draw in a tail, udder, and markings. Add grass.

you can do it!
Use crayons for texture and paint over with watercolor paint. Use a felt-tip marker for the lines.

Splat-a-fact
No two cows have the same markings or spots.

Donkey

1 Draw a bean shape with a dot for the eye.

2 Add nostrils and a mouth.

3 Add ears, a neck, and a mane.

4 Draw in a curved body and a tail.

5 Add four legs and hooves.

you can do it!
Use a black felt-tip marker for the lines and add color using colored felt-tip markers.

8

Mallard

you can do it!

Use oil pastels and smudge them with your finger. Use a felt-tip marker for the lines.

1 Start with the head and add a dot for the eye.

2 Draw in the beak.

splat-a-fact

Mallards have webbed feet designed for swimming.

3 Draw in the body with a pointed tail. Add a curved line for the wing and across the chest.

4 Add legs with webbed feet and a zig-zag line around the neck.

Farm cat

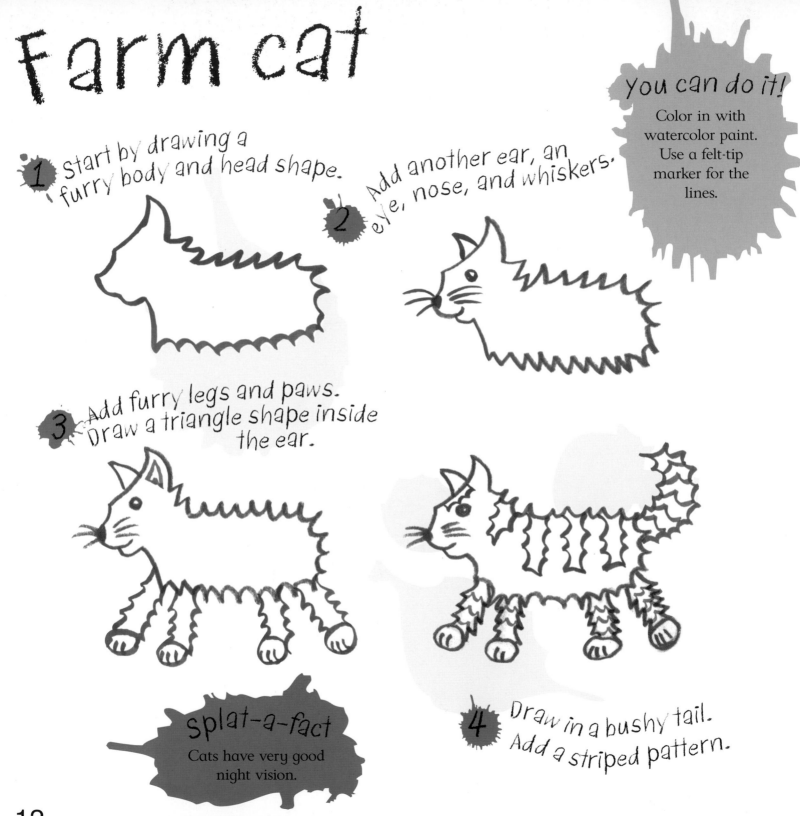

12

1 Start by drawing a furry body and head shape.

2 Add another ear, an eye, nose, and whiskers.

you can do it!
Color in with watercolor paint. Use a felt-tip marker for the lines.

3 Add furry legs and paws. Draw a triangle shape inside the ear.

splat-a-fact
Cats have very good night vision.

4 Draw in a bushy tail. Add a striped pattern.

Goat

1 Start with the head.

2 Draw in ears, eyes, and a nose.

3 Add two horns, a neck, and a beard.

splat-a-fact
Goats have four stomachs.

4 Draw in the body and tail.

You can do it!
Use crayons for all textures and paint over with watercolor paint. Use a blue felt-tip marker for the lines.

5 Add the legs and hooves.

14

Duck

1 Start with the body shape and tail feathers.

2 Add the beak.

3 Draw in two webbed feet.

4 Add eyes and a wing. Finish with the beak details.

you can do it!
Use colored pencils and a felt-tip marker for the lines. Use pencils in a scribbly way so the color looks more interesting.

Horse

you can do it!
Use colored pencils and a felt-tip marker for the lines. Color in a scribbly way to add texture.

1 Start with the head.

2 Add nostrils, a mouth, and a dot for an eye.

splat-a-fact

Horses sleep standing up!

3 Draw in the horse's neck, ears, and mane.

4 Add a bean-shaped body and a tail.

5 Draw in four legs and hooves.

18

Owl

1 Start with the head shape. Add a curved line for detail.

2 Draw in the eyes and a beak.

you can do it!
Tear up colored tissue paper and glue it down for the color. Use a felt-tip marker for the lines.

3 Draw the body shape and a fan-shaped tail.

4 Add two large pointed wings.

5 Add two legs and feet.

Splat-a-fact

Barn owls do not hoot— they screech!

20

Pig

1 Start with the head. Add an oval for the nose.

2 Add the ears, eyes, nostrils, and a mouth.

4 Draw in a curly tail and add spotted markings.

3 Add the body.

Splat-a-fact
Some pigs have tusks to fight with and dig for food.

5 Add four legs and feet.

22

Rabbit

1 Start with a circle for the head and an oval for the body.

2 Add the eyes, teeth, a nose, mouth, and whiskers.

you can do it!
Draw in the lines with a brown felt-tip marker. Use colored pencils to add color.

3 Add four legs.

4 Add a tail and ears.

splat-a-fact
There are about 25 different species of rabbit.

Sheep

1 Start with a fluffy body.

2 Draw in the head shape with a fluffy top and add ears.

3 Draw two dots for eyes, nostrils, and grass.

you can do it!
Use watercolor paint to color. Use a sponge to dab on the paint for added texture.

4 Draw in four legs and feet and add a tail.

Sheepdog

splat-a-fact

Sheepdogs help farmers to round up sheep.

1 Start by cutting out the shape of the body.

2 Cut out another furry shape and glue down.

3 Draw in the eyes, nose, tongue, and outline.

you can do it!
Cut the shapes out of colored paper and glue in place. The dog's head must overlap the body.

4 Cut out more fur for the head and glue down.

Turkey

1 Start with a big curl to make an oval-shaped body.

2 Add fan-shaped feathers.

3 Draw two legs and spiky feet.

4 Draw in a neck and head. Add a beak and a dot for the eye. Add head details and zig-zag lines for the tail feathers.

30

Index